BELIEVE

Because you are but a young man, beware of temptations and snares; and above all, be careful to keep yourself in the use of means; resort to good company; and howbeit you be nicknamed a Puritan, and mocked, yet care not for that, but rejoice and be glad, that they who are scorned and scoffed by this godless and vain world, and nicknamed Puritans, would admit you to their society; for I must tell you, when I am at this point as you see me, I get no comfort to my soul by any second means under heaven but from those who are nicknamed Puritans. They are the men that can give a word of comfort to a wearied soul in due season, and that I have found by experience . . .

THE LAST AND HEAVENLY SPEECHES, AND
GLORIOUS DEPARTURE, OF JOHN, VISCOUNT KENMURE

REPENT & BELIEVE

Thomas Brooks

Taken from
'Precious Remedies Against Satan's Devices',
The Works of Thomas Brooks, Vol. 1

THE BANNER OF TRUTH TRUST

THE BANNER OF TRUTH TRUST
3 Murrayfield Road, Edinburgh EH12 6EL, UK
P.O. Box 621, Carlisle, PA 17013, USA

*

© The Banner of Truth Trust 2008

ISBN: 978 1 84871 019 1

*

Typeset in 10.5 / 13.5 pt Adobe Caslon Pro
at the Banner of Truth Trust, Edinburgh

Printed in the USA by
Versa Press, Inc.,
East Peoria, IL

*

Minor editorial adjustments have been made to the
original text, e.g. the modernizing of some words
and the supply of Scripture references.

Repent & Believe

Satan's Device—Repentance is Easy!

Satan persuades the soul that the work of repentance is an easy work, and that therefore the soul need not worry too much about the matter of sin.

Why! Suppose you do sin, says Satan, it is no such difficult thing to return, and confess, and be sorrowful, and beg pardon, and cry, 'Lord, have mercy upon me!' and if you do but this, God will cut the score, and pardon your sins, and save your souls. By this device Satan draws many a soul to sin, and makes many millions of souls servants or rather slaves to sin.

Remedy 1.

The first remedy is, seriously to consider, That repentance is a mighty work, a difficult work, a work that is above our power.

There is no power below that power that raised Christ from the dead, and that made the world, that can break the heart of a sinner or turn the heart of a sinner. You are as well able to melt adamant, as to melt your own heart; to turn a flint into flesh, as to turn your own heart to the Lord; to raise the dead and to make a world, as to repent. Repentance is a flower that grows not in nature's garden. 'Can the Ethiopian change his skin, or the leopard his spots? then may ye also do good, that are accustomed to do evil' (*Jer.* 13:23). Repentance is a gift that comes down from above. Men are not born with repentance in their hearts, as they are born with tongues in their mouths: Acts 5:31: 'Him hath God exalted with his right hand to be a Prince and a Saviour, for to give repentance to Israel, and forgiveness of sins.' So in 2 Timothy 2:25: 'In meekness instructing them that oppose themselves; if God peradventure will give them repentance to the acknowledging of the truth'. It is not in the power of any mortal to repent at pleasure. Some ignorant deluded souls vainly conceive that these five words, *'Lord! have mercy upon me'*, are efficacious to send them to heaven; but as many are undone by buying a counterfeit jewel, so many are in hell by mistake of their repentance. Many rest in their repentance, though it may be but the shadow of repentance, which caused one to say, 'Repentance damneth more than sin.'

REMEDY 2.

The second remedy against this device of Satan is, solemnly to consider the nature of true repentance.

Repentance is some other thing than what vain men conceive.

Repentance is sometimes taken, in a more strict and narrow sense, for godly sorrow; sometimes repentance is taken, in a large sense, for amendment of life. Repentance has in it three things, *viz.*: the act, subject, terms.

(1.) *The formal act of repentance is a changing and converting*. It is often set forth in Scripture by turning. 'Turn thou me, and I shall be turned', says Ephraim; 'after that I was turned, I repented', says he (*Jer.* 31:18, 19). It is a turning from darkness to light.

(2.) *The subject changed and converted is the whole man*: it is both the sinner's heart and life: first his heart, then his life; first his person, then his practice and conversation. 'Wash you, make you clean': there is the change of their persons; 'Put away the evil of your doings from before mine eyes; cease to do evil, learn to do well' (*Isa.* 1:16-17); there is the change of their practices. So 'Cast away', says Ezekiel, 'all your transgressions whereby you have transgressed'; there is the change of the life; 'and make you a new heart and a new spirit' (*Ezek.* 18:31); there is the change of the heart.

(3.) *The terms of this change and conversion, from which and to which both heart and life must be changed; from sin to God.* The heart must be changed from the state and power of sin, the life from the acts of sin, but both unto God; the heart to be under his power in a state of grace, the life to be under his rule in all new obedience; as the apostle speaks: 'To open their eyes and to turn them from darkness to light, and from the power of Satan unto God' (*Acts* 26:18). So the prophet Isaiah says, 'Let the wicked forsake his way, and the unrighteous man his thoughts, and let him return unto the Lord' (*Isa.* 55:7).

Thus much of the nature of evangelical repentance. Now, souls, tell me whether it be such an easy thing to repent, as Satan suggests. Besides what has been spoken, I desire that you will take notice, that repentance includes turning from the most darling sin. 'Ephraim shall say, What have I to do any more with idols?' (*Hos.* 14:8). Yea, it is a turning from all sin to God: 'Therefore I will judge you, O house of Israel, every one according to his ways, saith the Lord God. Repent, and turn yourselves from all your transgressions; so iniquity shall not be your ruin (*Ezek.* 18:30). Herod turned from many, but turned not from his Herodias, which was his ruin. Judas turned from all visible wickedness, yet he would not cast out that golden devil covetousness, and therefore was cast into the hottest place in hell. He that turns not from every sin, turns not aright from any one sin. Every sin strikes at the honour of God, the being of God, the glory of God, the heart of Christ, the joy of the Spirit, and the peace of a man's conscience; and therefore a soul truly penitent strikes at all, hates all, conflicts with all, and will labour to draw strength from a crucified Christ to crucify all. A true penitent knows neither father nor mother, neither right eye nor right hand, but will pluck out the one and cut off the other. Saul spared but one, King Agag, and that cost him his soul and his kingdom (1 *Sam.* 15:9).

Besides, repentance is not only a turning from all sin, but also a turning to all good; to a love of all good, to a prizing of all good, and to a following after all good: 'But if the wicked will turn from all his sins that he hath committed, and keep all my statutes, and do that which is lawful and right, he shall surely live, he shall not die' (*Ezek.* 18:21); that is, only negative righteousness and holiness is no righteousness nor holiness. David fulfilled *all* the will of God, and had respect unto *all* his commandments, and so had Zacharias and Elizabeth. It is not enough that the tree does not bear bad fruit; but it must bring forth good fruit, else it must be 'cut down and cast into the fire' (*Luke* 13:7; cf. *Matt.* 7:19). So it is not enough that you are not thus and thus wicked, but you must be thus and thus gracious and good, else divine justice will put the axe of divine vengeance to the root of your souls, and cut you off for ever. 'Every tree that bringeth not forth good fruit is hewed down and cast into the fire' (*Matt.* 3:10).

Besides, repentance includes a felt sense of sin's sinfulness, how opposite and contrary it is to the blessed God. God is light, sin is darkness; God is life, sin is death; God is heaven, sin is hell; God is beauty, sin is deformity.

Also true repentance includes a felt sense of sin's mischievousness; how it cast angels out of heaven, and Adam out of paradise; how it laid the first corner stone in hell, and brought in all the curses, crosses, and miseries, that be in the world; and how it makes men liable to all temporal, spiritual and eternal wrath; how it has made men godless, Christless, hopeless, and heavenless.

Further, true repentance includes sorrow for sin, contrition of heart. It breaks the heart with sighs, and sobs, and groans, for that a loving God and Father is by sin offended, a blessed Saviour afresh crucified, and the sweet Comforter, the Spirit, grieved and vexed.

Again, repentance includes, not only a loathing of sin, but also a loathing of ourselves for sin. As a man does not only loathe poison, but he loathes the very dish or vessel that has the smell of the poison; so a true penitent does not only loathe his sin, but he loathes himself, the vessel that smells of it; so Ezekiel 20:43: 'And there shall ye remember your ways and all your doings, wherein ye have been defiled; and ye shall loathe yourselves in your own sight for all your evils that ye have committed.' True repentance will work your hearts, not only to loathe your sins, but to loathe yourselves.

Again, true repentance does not only work a man to loathe himself for his sins, but it makes him ashamed of his sin also: 'What fruit had ye in those things whereof ye are now ashamed?' says the apostle

(*Rom.* 6:21), So Ezekiel: 'And thou shalt be confounded, and never open thy mouth any more, because of thy shame, when I am pacified toward thee for all that thou hast done, saith the Lord God' (*Ezek.* 16:63). When a penitent soul sees his sins pardoned, the anger of God pacified, the divine justice satisfied, then he sits down and blushes, as the Hebrew has it, as one ashamed. Yea, true repentance works a man to cross his sinful self, and to walk contrary to sinful self, to take a holy revenge upon sin, as you may see in Paul, the Philippian jailor, Mary Magdalene, and Manasseh. This the apostle shows in 2 Corinthians 7: 10-11: 'For godly sorrow worketh repentance never to be repented of; but the sorrow of the world worketh death. For behold the self-same thing, that ye sorrowed after a godly sort, what carefulness it wrought in you, yea, what clearing of yourselves, yea, what indignation, yea, what fear, yea, what vehement desire, yea, what zeal, yea, what revenge.'

Now souls, sum up all these things together, and tell me whether it would be such an easy thing to repent as Satan would make the soul to believe, and I am confident your heart will answer that it is as hard a thing to repent as it is to make a world, or raise the dead.

I shall conclude this second remedy with a worthy saying of a precious holy man: 'Repentance strips us stark naked of all the garments of the old Adam, and leaves not so much as a shirt behind.' In this rotten building it leaves not a stone upon a stone. As the flood drowned Noah's own friends and servants, so must the flood of repenting tears drown our sweetest and most profitable sins.

REMEDY 3.

The third remedy against this device of Satan is seriously to consider, that repentance is a continued act.

The word repent implies the continuation of it. True repentance inclines a man's heart to perform God's statutes always, even unto the end. A true penitent must go on from faith to faith, from strength to strength; he must never stand still nor turn back. Repentance is a grace, and must have its daily operation as well as other graces. True repentance is a continued spring, where the waters of godly sorrow are always flowing: 'My sin is ever before me' (*Psa.* 51:3). A true penitent is often casting his eyes back to the days of his former vanity, and this makes him morning and evening to 'water his couch with his tears'. 'Remember not against me the sins of my youth', said one blessed penitent; and 'I was a blasphemer, and a persecutor, and injurious', said another penitent.

Repentance is a continued act of turning, a repentance never to be repented of, a turning never to turn again to folly. A true penitent has ever something within him to turn from; he can never get near enough to God; no, not so near him as once he was; and therefore he is still turning and turning that he may get nearer and nearer to him; that is his chiefest good and his only happiness, *optimum maximum*, the best and the greatest. They are every day crying out, 'O wretched men that we are, who shall deliver us from this body of death!' (*Rom.* 7:24). They are still sensitive to sin, and still conflicting with sin, and still sorrowing for sin, and still loathing of themselves for sin.

Repentance is no transient act, but a continued act of the soul. And tell me, O tempted soul, whether it be such an easy thing as Satan would make you believe, to be every day turning more and more from sin, and turning nearer and nearer to God, your choicest blessedness. A true penitent can as easily content himself with one act of faith, or one act of love, as he can content himself with one act of repentance.

A Jewish Rabbi, pressing the practice of repentance upon his disciples, and exhorting them to be sure to repent the day before they died, one of them replied, that the day of any man's death was very uncertain. 'Repent, therefore, every day', said the Rabbi, 'and then you shall be sure to repent the day before you die.' You are wise, and know how to apply it to your own advantage.

REMEDY 4.

The fourth remedy against this device of Satan is solemnly to consider, that if the work of repentance were such an easy work as Satan would make it to be, then certainly so many would not lie roaring and crying out of wrath and eternal ruin under the horrors and terrors of conscience, for not repenting; yea, doubtless, so many millions would not go to hell for not repenting, if it were such an easy thing to repent.

Ah, do not poor souls under horror of conscience cry out and say, 'Were all this world a lump of gold, and in our hand to dispose of, we would give it for the least penny of true repentance!' and wilt you say it is an easy thing to repent? When a poor sinner, whose conscience is awakened, shall judge the exchange of all the world for the least penny of repentance to be the happiest exchange that ever sinner made, tell me, O soul, is it good going to hell? Is it good dwelling with the devouring fire, with everlasting burnings? Is it good to be for ever separated from the blessed and glorious presence of God, and saints, and to be for ever shut out from those good things of eternal life, which are so many that they exceed number; so great, that they exceed measure; so precious, that they exceed all estimation? We know it is the greatest misery that can befall the sons of men; and would they not prevent this by repentance, if it were such an easy thing to repent as Satan would have it?

Well, then, do not run the hazard of losing God, Christ, heaven, and your soul for ever, by hearkening to this device of Satan, *viz.*, that it is an easy thing to repent.

If it be so easy, why, then, do wicked men's hearts so rise against them that press the doctrine of repentance in the sweetest way, and by the strongest and the choicest arguments that the Scripture affords? And why do they kill two at once: the faithful labourer's name and their own souls, by their wicked words and actings, because they are put upon repenting, which Satan tells them is so easy a thing? Surely, were repentance so easy, wicked men would not be so much enraged when that doctrine is, by evangelical considerations, pressed upon them.

Remedy 5.

The fifth remedy against this device of Satan is seriously to consider, that to repent of sin is as great a work of grace as not to sin.

By our sinful falls the powers of the soul are weakened, the strength of grace is decayed, our evidences for heaven are blotted, fears and doubts in the soul are raised (will God once more pardon this scarlet sin, and show mercy to this wretched soul?), and corruptions in the heart are more advantaged and confirmed; and the conscience of a man after falls is the more enraged or the more benumbed. Now for a soul, notwith-standing all this, to repent of his falls, this shows that it is as great a work of grace to repent of sin as it is not to sin.

Repentance is the vomit of the soul; and of all remedies, none so difficult and hard as it is to vomit. The same means that tends to preserve the soul from sin, the same means works the soul to rise by repentance when it is fallen into sin. We know the mercy and loving-kindness of God is one special means to keep the soul from sin; as David spoke, 'Thy loving-kindness is always before mine eyes, and I have walked in thy truth, and I have not sat with vain persons, neither will I go in with dis-semblers. I have hated the congregation of evil doers, and will not sit with the wicked' (*Psa.* 26:3-5). So by the same means the soul is raised by repentance out of sin, as you may see in Mary Magdalene, who loved much, and wept much, because much was forgiven her (*Luke* 7:37-50). So those in Hosea: 'Come, let us return unto the Lord; for he hath torn, and he will heal; he hath smitten, and he will bind us up. After two days he will revive us, in the third day he will raise us up, and we shall live in his sight [or before his face]' (*Hos.* 6:1-2); as the Hebrew has it, 'in his favour'. Confidence in God's mercy and love, that he would heal them, and bind up their wounds, and revive their dejected spirits, and cause them to live in his favour, was that which did work their hearts to repent and return unto him.

I might further show you this truth in many other particulars, but this may suffice: only remember this in the general, that there is as much of the power of God, and love of God, and faith in God, and fear of God, and care to please God, zeal for the glory of God (2 *Cor.* 7:11) requisite to work a man to repent of sin, as there is to keep a man from sin; by which you may easily judge, that to repent of sin is as great a work as not to sin. And now tell me, O soul, is it an easy thing not to sin? We know then certainly it is not an easy thing to repent of sin.

REMEDY 6.

The sixth remedy against this device of Satan is, seriously to consider, that he that now tempts thee to sin upon this account, that repentance is easy, will, before long, to cause you to despair, and for ever to break the neck of your soul, present repentance as the most difficult and hardest work in the world.

And to this purpose he will set your sins in order before you, and make them to say, 'We are yours, and we must follow you.'

Now, Satan will help to work the soul to look up, and see God angry; and to look inward, and to see conscience accusing and condemning; and to look downwards, and see hell's mouth open to receive the impenitent soul: and all this to render the work of repentance impossible to the soul. What, says Satan, do you think that that is easy which the whole power of grace cannot conquer while we are in this world? Is it easy, says Satan, to turn from some outward act of sin to which you have been addicted? Do you not remember that you have often complained against such and such particular sins, and resolved to leave them, and yet, to this hour, you have not, you cannot? What will it then be to turn from every sin? Yea, to mortify and cut off those sins, those darling lusts, that are as joints and members, that be as right hands and right eyes? Have you not loved your sins above your Saviour? Have you not preferred earth before heaven? Have you not all along neglected the means of grace and despised the offers of grace and vexed the Spirit of grace?

There would be no end, if I should set before you the infinite evils that you have committed, and the innumerable good services that you have omitted, and the frequent checks of your own conscience that you have despised; and therefore you may well conclude that you can never repent, that you shall never repent.

Now, says Satan, do but a little consider your numberless sins, and the greatness of your sins, the foulness of your sins, the heinousness of your sins, the circumstances of your sins, and you shall easily see that those sins that you thought to be but motes, are indeed mountains; and is it not now in vain to repent of them? Surely, says Satan, if you should seek repentance and grace with tears, as Esau, you shall not find it; your hour glass is out, your sun is set, the door of mercy is shut, the golden sceptre is taken in, and now you that have despised mercy, shall be for ever destroyed by justice. For such a wretch as you are to attempt repentance is to attempt a thing impossible. It is impossible that you, that in all your life could never conquer one sin, should master such a numberless number of sins, which are so near, so dear, so necessary, and so profitable to you, that have so long bedded and boarded with you, that have been old acquaintances and companions with you. Have you not often purposed, promised, vowed, and resolved to enter upon the practice of repentance, but to this day could never attain it? Surely it is in vain to strive against the stream, where it is so impossible to overcome; you are lost and cast away for ever; to hell you must, to hell you shall, go.

Ah, souls! he that now tempts you to sin, by suggesting to you the easiness of repentance, will at last cause you to despair, and present repentance as the hardest work in all the world, and a work as far above man as heaven is above hell, as light is above darkness. Oh that you were wise, to break of your sins by timely repentance.

SATAN'S DEVICES TO STOP SINNERS
BELIEVING ON JESUS CHRIST

Touching five more devices of Satan, whereby he keepeth poor souls from believing in Christ, from receiving of Christ, from embracing of Christ, from resting, leaning, or relying upon Christ, for everlasting happiness and blessedness, according to the gospel; and remedies against these devices.

Device 1.

BY SUGGESTING TO THE SOUL THE GREATNESS AND VILENESS OF HIS SINS.

What! says Satan, do you think you shall ever obtain mercy by Christ—you who have sinned with so high a hand against Christ, who have slighted the offers of grace, who have grieved the Spirit of grace, who have despised the word of grace, who have trampled under feet the blood of the covenant by which you might have been pardoned, purged, justified, and saved, who have spoken and done all the evil that you could? No! no! says Satan, he has mercy for others, but not for you; pardon for others, but not for you; righteousness for others, but not for you. Therefore it is in vain for you to think of believing in Christ, or resting and leaning your guilty soul upon Christ (Jer. 3:5).

The first remedy against this device of Satan is to consider, that the greater your sins are, the more you stand in need of a Saviour.

The greater your burden is, the more you stand in need of one to help to bear it. The deeper the wound is, the more need there is of the surgeon; the more dangerous the disease is, the more need there is of the physician. Who but madmen will argue thus: My burden is great, therefore I will not call out for help; my wound is deep, therefore I will not call out for balm; my disease is dangerous, therefore I will not go to the physician. Ah! it is spiritual madness, it is the devil's logic to argue thus: My sins are great, therefore I will not go to Christ, I dare not rest nor lean on Christ; whereas the soul should reason thus: The greater my sins are, the more I stand in need of mercy, of pardon, and therefore I will go to Christ, who delights in mercy, who pardons sin for his own name's sake, who is as able and as willing to forgive pounds as pence, thousands as hundreds (*Mic.* 7:18; *Isa.* 43:25).

REMEDY 2.

The second remedy against this device of Satan is, solemnly to consider, that the promise of grace and mercy is to returning souls.

And, therefore, though you are never so wicked, yet if you will return, God will be yours, and mercy shall be yours, and pardon shall be yours: 'For if you turn again unto the Lord, your brethren and your children shall find compassion before them that lead them captive, so that they shall come again into this land: for the Lord our God is gracious and merciful, and will not turn away his face from you, if ye return unto him' (2 *Chron.* 30:9) So Jeremiah 3:12: 'Go and proclaim these words towards the north, and say, Return, thou backsliding Israel, saith the Lord, and I will not cause my anger to fall upon you: for I am merciful, saith the Lord, and I will not keep anger for ever.' So Joel 2:13: 'And rend your hearts, and not your garments, and turn unto the Lord your God: for he is gracious and merciful, slow to anger, and of great kindness, and repenteth him of the evil.' So Isaish 55:7: 'Let the wicked forsake his ways, and the unrighteous man his thoughts: and let him return unto the Lord, and he will have mercy upon him; and to our God, for he will abundantly pardon': or, as the Hebrew reads it, 'He will multiply pardon.' So Ezekiel 18.

Ah! sinner, it is not your great transgressions that shall exclude you from mercy, if you will break off your sins by repentance and return to the fountain of mercy. Christ's heart, Christ's arms, are wide open to embrace the returning prodigal. It is not simply the greatness of your sins, but your peremptory persisting in sin, that will be your eternal overthrow.

Remedy 3.

The third remedy against this device of Satan is, solemnly to consider, that the greatest sinners have obtained mercy, and therefore all the angels in heaven, all the men on earth, and all the devils in hell cannot tell to the contrary, but that you may obtain mercy.

Manasseh was a notorious sinner; he erected altars for Baal, he worshipped and served all the host of heaven; he caused his sons to pass through the fire; he gave himself to witchcraft and sorcery; he made Judah to sin more wickedly than the heathen did, whom the Lord destroyed before the children of Israel; he caused the streets of Jerusalem to run down with innocent blood (2 *Kings* 21). Ah! what a devil incarnate was he in his actions! Yet when he humbled himself, and sought the Lord. the Lord was entreated of him and heard his supplication, and brought him to Jerusalem, and made himself known unto him, and crowned him with mercy and loving-kindness, as you may see in 2 Chronicles 33:12-13.

So Paul was once a blasphemer, a persecutor and injurious, yet he obtained mercy (1 *Tim.* 1:13).

So Mary Magdalene was a notorious strumpet, a common whore, out of whom Christ cast seven devils, yet she is pardoned by Christ, and dearly beloved of Christ (*Luke* 7:37-38). So Mark 16:9: 'Now, when Jesus was risen early the first day of the week, he appeared first to Mary Magdalene, out of whom he had cast seven devils.'

Jansenius on the place says, it is very observable that our Saviour after his resurrection first appeared to Mary Magdalene and Peter, that had been grievous sinners; that even the worst of sinners may be comforted and encouraged to come to Christ, to believe in Christ, to rest and stay their souls upon Christ, for mercy here and glory hereafter. That is a very precious word for the worst of sinners to hang upon, Psalm 68:18. The psalmist speaking of Christ says:

'Thou hast ascended on high, thou hast led led captivity captive; thou hast received gifts for men; yea, for the rebellious also, that the Lord might dwell amongst them.'

What though you are a rebellious child, or a rebellious servant! What though you are a rebellious swearer, a rebellious drunkard, a rebellious Sabbath breaker! Yet Christ has received gifts for you, 'even for the rebellious also'. He has received the gift of pardon, the gift of righteousness, yea, all the gifts of the Spirit for you, that your heart may be made a delightful house for God to dwell in.

John Bodin has a story concerning a great rebel that had made a strong party against a Roman emperor. The emperor makes proclamation, that whoever could bring the rebel dead or alive, he should have such a great sum of money. The rebel hearing of this, comes and presents himself before the emperor, and demands the sum of money. Now, says the emperor, if I should put him to death, the world would say I did it to save my money. And so he pardons the rebel, and gives him the money.

Ah! sinners! Shall a heathen do this, that had but a drop of mercy and compassion in him: and will not Christ do much more, that has all fullness of grace, mercy, and glory in himself? Surely his heart yearns towards the worst of rebels. Ah! if you still but come in, you will find him ready to pardon, yea, one made up of pardoning mercy. Oh! the readiness and willingness of Jesus Christ to receive to favour the greatest rebels! The father of mercies met, embraced, and kissed that prodigal mouth which came from feeding with swine and kissing of harlots (cf. *Col.* 1:19; 2:3-4).

Ephraim had committed idolatry, and was backslidden from God; he was guilty of lukewarmness and unbelief, &c., yet says God, 'Ephraim is my dear son, he is a pleasant child, my bowels [heart] are troubled for him, I will have mercy', or rather as it is in the original, 'I will have mercy, mercy upon him, saith the Lord.'

Well! says God, though Ephraim be guilty of crimson sins, yet he is a son, a dear son, a precious son, a pleasant child; though he be black with filth, and red with guilt, yet my heart is troubled for him; I will have mercy, mercy upon him. Ah sinners, if this heart of mercy does not melt, win, and draw you, justice will be a swift witness against you, and make you lie down in eternal misery for kicking against the heart of mercy.

Christ hangs out still, as once that warlike Scythian did, a white flag of grace and mercy to returning sinners that humble themselves at his feet for favour; but if sinners stand out, Christ will put forth his red flag, his bloody flag, and they shall die for ever by a hand of justice. Sinners! there is no way to avoid perishing by Christ's iron rod, but by kissing his golden sceptre.

REMEDY 4.

The fourth remedy against this device of Satan is, to consider, that Jesus Christ has nowhere in all the Scripture made an exception against the worst of sinners that are willing to receive him, to believe in him, to rest upon him for happiness and blessedness.

Ah! sinners, why should you be more cruel and unmerciful to your own souls than Christ is? Christ has not excluded you from mercy, why should you exclude your own souls from mercy? Oh that you would dwell often upon that choice Scripture (*John* 6:37): 'All that the Father giveth me shall come to me; and him that cometh to me I will in no wise cast out': or as the original has it, 'I will not not cast out.' Well! saith Christ, if any man will come, or is coming to me, let him be more sinful or less; more unworthy or less; let him be never so guilty, never so filthy, never so rebellious, never so leprous, yet if he will but come, I will not not cast him off.

So much is held forth in 1 Corinthians 6:9-11: 'Know ye not that the unrighteous shall not inherit the kingdom of God?

Be not deceived: neither fornicators, nor idolaters, nor adulterers, nor effeminate, nor abusers of themselves with mankind, nor thieves, nor covetous, nor drunkards, nor revilers, nor extortioners, shall inherit the kingdom of God. And such were some of you: but ye are washed, but ye are sanctified, but ye are justified, in the name of the Lord Jesus, and by the Spirit of our God.'

Ah! sinners, do not think that he who has received such notorious sinners to mercy will reject you. 'He is yesterday, and today, and for ever the same' (*Heb.* 13:8). Christ was born in an inn, to show that he receives all comers; his garments were divided into four parts, to show that out of whatever part of the world we come, we shall be received. If we be naked, Christ has robes to clothe us; if we be homeless, Christ has room to lodge us. That is a choice scripture (*Acts* 10:34-35): 'Then Peter opened his mouth and said, Of a truth I perceive that God is no respecter of persons. But in every nation, he that feareth him, and worketh righteousness, is accepted with him.'

The three tongues that were written upon the cross, Greek, Latin, and Hebrew (*John* 19:19-20), to witness Christ to be the king of the Jews, do each of them in their several idioms avouch this singular axiom, that Christ is an all-sufficient Saviour; and 'a threefold cord is not easily broken.' The apostle puts this out of doubt: 'Wherefore he is able also to save them to the uttermost that come unto God by him, seeing he ever liveth to make intercession for them' (*Heb.* 7:25).

Now, he were not an all-sufficient Saviour if he were not able to save the greatest, as well as the least of sinners. Ah! sinners, tell Jesus Christ that he has not excluded you from mercy, and therefore you are resolved that you will sit, wait, weep, and knock at the door of mercy, till he shall say, Souls, be of good cheer, your sins are forgiven, your persons are justified, and your souls shall be saved.

REMEDY 5.

The fifth remedy against this device of Satan is, to consider, that the greater sinner you are, the dearer you will be to Christ, when he shall behold you as the travail of his soul (Isa. 53:11): 'He shall see of the travail of his soul, and be satisfied.'

The dearer we pay for anything, the dearer that thing is to us. Christ has paid most, and prayed most, and sighed most, and wept most, and bled most for the greatest sinners, and therefore they are dearer to Christ than others that are less sinful. Rachel was dearer to Jacob than Leah, because she cost him more; he obeyed, endured, and suffered more by day and night for her than for Leah.

Ah! sinners, the greatness of your sins does but set off the freeness and riches of Christ's grace, and the freeness of his love. This makes heaven and earth to ring of his praise, that he loves those that are most unlovely, that he shows most favour to them that have sinned most highly against him, as might be showed by several instances in Scripture, as Paul, Mary Magdalene, and others. Who sinned more against Christ than these? And who had sweeter and choicer manifestations of divine love and favour than these?

REMEDY 6.

The sixth remedy against this device of Satan is seriously to consider, that the longer you keep off from Christ, the greater and stronger your sins will grow.

All divine power and strength against sin flows from the soul's union and communion with Christ (*Rom.* 8:10; 1 *John* 1:6-7). While you keep off from Christ, you keep off from that strength and power which is alone able to make you trample down strength, lead captivity captive, and slay the Goliaths that bid defiance to Christ. It is only faith in Christ that makes a man triumph over sin, Satan, hell, and the world (1 *John* 5:4). It is only faith in Christ that binds the strong man's hand and foot, that stops the issue of blood, that makes a man strong in resisting, and happy in conquering. Sin always dies most where faith lives most. The most believing soul is the most mortified soul.

Ah! sinner, remember this, there is no way on earth effectually to be rid of the guilt, filth, and power of sin, but by believing in a Saviour. It is not resolving, it is not complaining, it is not mourning, but believing, that will make you divinely victorious over that body of sin that to this day is too strong for you, and that will certainly be your ruin, if it be not ruined by a hand of faith.

REMEDY 7.

The seventh remedy against this device of Satan is, wisely to consider, that as there is nothing in Christ to discourage the greatest sinners from believing in him, so there is everything

in Christ that may encourage the greatest sin-
ners to believe on him, to rest and lean upon
him for all happiness and blessedness (Song of
Sol. 1:3*).*

If you look upon his nature, his disposition, his names, his titles, his offices as king, priest, and prophet, you will find nothing to discourage the greatest sinners from believing in him, but many things to encourage the greatest sinners to receive him, to believe in him. Christ is the greatest good, the choicest good, the chiefest good, the most suitable good, the most necessary good. He is a pure good, a real good, a total good, an eternal good, and a soul-satisfying good.

Revelation 3:17-18: Sinners, are you poor? Christ has gold to enrich you. Are you naked? Christ has royal robes, he has white garments to clothe you. Are you blind? Christ has eye-salve to enlighten you. Are you hungry? Christ will be manna to feed you. Are you thirsty? He will be a well of living water to refresh you. Are you wounded? He has a balm under his wings to heal you. Are you sick? He is a physician to cure you. Are you prisoners? He has laid down a ransom for you.

Ah, sinners! tell me, tell me, is there anything in Christ to keep you off from believing? No! Is there not everything in Christ that may encourage you to believe in him? Yes! Oh, then, believe in him and then, 'Though your sins be as scarlet, they shall be as white as snow, though they be red like crimson, they shall be as wool' (*Isa.* 1:18). Nay, then, your iniquities shall be forgotten as well as forgiven, they shall be remembered no more. God will cast them behind his back, he will throw them into the bottom of the sea (*Isa.* 43:25; 38:17; *Mic.* 7:19).

REMEDY 8.

The eighth remedy against this device of Satan is, seriously to consider, The absolute necessity of believing in Christ.

Heaven is too holy and too hot to hold unbelievers; their lodging is prepared in hell: 'But the fearful and unbelieving &c. shall have their part in the lake which burneth with fire and brimstone. which is the second death' (*Rev.* 21:8). 'If ye believe not that I am he', says Christ, 'you shall die in your sins' (*John* 8:24). And he that dies in his sins must go to judgment and to hell in his sins. Every unbeliever is a condemned man: 'He that believeth not', says John, 'is condemned already, because he hath not believed in the name of the only begotten Son of God. And he that believeth not the Son, shall not see life, but the wrath of God abideth on him' (*John* 3:18, 36).

Ah, sinners! the law, the gospel, and your own consciences, have passed the sentence of condemnation upon you, and there is no way to reverse the sentence but by believing in Christ. And therefore my counsel is this, Stir up yourselves to lay hold on the Lord Jesus, and look up to him, and wait on him, from whom every good and perfect gift comes, and give him no rest till he has given you that jewel faith, that is more worth than heaven and earth, and that will make you happy in life, joyful in death, and glorious in the day of Christ (*Isa.* 64. 7; *James* 1:17; *Isa.* 62:7).

And thus much for the remedies against this first device of Satan, whereby he keeps off thousands from believing in Christ.

Device 2.

BY SUGGESTING TO SINNERS THEIR UNWORTHINESS.

Ah! says Satan, as you are worthy of the greatest misery, so you are unworthy of the least crumb of mercy. What! do you think, says Satan, that ever Christ will own, receive, or embrace such an unworthy wretch as you are? No, no; if there were any worthiness in you, then, indeed, Christ might be willing to be entertained by you. You are unworthy to entertain Christ into your house, how much more unworthy are you to entertain Christ into your heart.

REMEDY 1.

The first remedy against this device of Satan is, seriously to consider, that God has nowhere in the Scripture required any worthiness in the creature before believing in Christ.

If you make a diligent search through all the Scripture, you shall not find, from the first line in Genesis to the last line in the Revelation, one word that speaks about God's requiring any worthiness in the creature before the soul's believing in Christ, before the soul's leaning and resting upon Christ for happiness and blessedness; and why, then, should that be a bar and hindrance to your faith, which God nowhere requires of you before you come to Christ, that you may have life? (*Matt.* 11:28; *John* 6:29). Ah, sinners! remember Satan objects your unworthiness against you only out of a design to keep Christ and your souls asunder for ever; and therefore, in the face of all your unworthiness, rest upon Christ, come to Christ, believe in Christ, and you are happy for ever (*John* 6:40, 47).

REMEDY 2.

The second remedy against this device of Satan is, wisely to consider, that none ever received Christ, embraced Christ, and obtained mercy and pardon from Christ, but unworthy souls.

I ask you, what worthiness was in Matthew, Zaccheus, Mary Magdalene, Manasseh, Paul, and Lydia, before their coming to Christ, before their faith in Christ? Surely none! Ah, sinners! you should reason thus: Christ has bestowed the choicest mercies, the greatest favours, the highest dignities, the sweetest privileges, upon unworthy sinners, and therefore, O our souls, don't you faint, don't you despair, but patiently and quietly wait for the salvation of the Lord. Who can tell but that free grace and mercy may shine forth upon us, though we are unworthy, and give us a portion among those worthies that are now triumphing in heaven.

REMEDY 3.

The third remedy against this device of Satan is, that if the soul will keep off from Christ till it be worthy, it will never close with Christ, it will never embrace Christ.

It will never be one with Christ, it must lie down in everlasting sorrow (*Isa.* 50:11). God has laid up all worthiness in Christ, that the creature may know where to find it, and may make out after it. There is no way on earth to make unworthy souls worthy, but by believing in Christ (*James* 2:23). Believing in Christ, of slaves, it will make you worthy sons; of enemies, it will make you worthy friends. God will count none worthy, nor call none worthy, nor behave towards none as worthy, but believers, who are made worthy by the worthiness of Christ's person, righteousness, satisfaction, and intercession (*Rev.* 3:4).

REMEDY 4.

The fourth remedy against this device of Satan is, solemnly to consider, That if you make a diligent search into your own hearts, you shall find that it is the pride and folly of your own hearts that puts you upon bringing of a worthiness to Christ.

Oh! you would gladly bring something to Christ that might render you acceptable to him; you are loathe to come empty-handed. The Lord cries out, 'Ho, every one that thirsteth, come ye to the waters, and he that hath no money: come ye, buy and eat; yea, come, buy wine and milk without money, and without price. Wherefore do ye spend your money upon that which is not bread, and your labour for that which satisfieth not?' (*Isa.* 55:1-2). Here the Lord calls upon moneyless, upon penniless souls, upon unworthy souls, to come and partake of his precious favours freely. But sinners are proud and foolish, and because they have no money, no worthiness to bring, they will not come, though he sweetly invites them.

Ah, sinners! what is more just than that you should perish for ever, that prefer husks among swine before the milk and wine, the sweet and precious things of the gospel, that are freely and sweetly offered to you. Well, sinners! remember this, it is not so much the sense of your unworthiness, as your pride, that keeps you off from a blessed closing with the Lord Jesus.

DEVICE 3.

BY SUGGESTING TO SINNERS THE WANT OF SUCH AND SUCH PREPARATIONS AND QUALIFICATIONS.

Satan says, 'You are not prepared to entertain Christ; you are not thus and thus humbled and justified; you are not heart-sick of sin; you have not been under horrors and terrors as such and such; you must stay till you are prepared and qualified to receive the Lord Jesus.'

Remedy 1.

The first remedy against this device of Satan is, solemnly to consider, that such as have not been so and so prepared and qualified as Satan suggests, have received Christ, believed in Christ, and been saved by Christ.

Matthew was called, sitting at the receipt of custom, and there was such power went along with Christ's call, that made him to follow him (*Matt.* 9:9). We read not of any horrors or terrors that he was under before his being called by Christ.

I ask you, what preparations and qualifications were found in Zacchæus, Paul, the Philippian jailor, and Lydia, before their conversion? (*Luke* 19.9; *Acts* 16:14, *seq.*). God brings in some by the sweet and still voice of the gospel, and usually such that are thus brought into Christ are the sweetest, humblest, choicest, and fruitfullest Christians.

God is a free agent to work by law or gospel, by smiles or frowns, by presenting hell or heaven to sinners' souls. God thunders from mount Sinai upon some souls, and conquers them by thundering. God speaks to others in a still voice, and by that conquers them. You that are brought to Christ by the law, do not judge and condemn them that are brought to Christ by the gospel; and you that are brought to Christ by the gospel, do not despise those that are brought to Christ by the law. Some are brought to Christ by fire, storms, and tempests, others by more easy and gentle gales of the Spirit. The Spirit is free in the works of conversion, and, as the wind, it blows when, where, and how it pleases (*John* 3:8). Thrice happy are those souls that are brought to Christ, whether it be in a winter's night or in a summer's day.

REMEDY 2.

The second remedy against this device of Satan is, solemnly to dwell upon these following scriptures, which do clearly evidence that poor sinners which are not so and so prepared and qualified to meet with Christ, to receive and embrace the Lord Jesus Christ, may, notwithstanding that, believe in Christ; and rest and lean upon him for happiness and blessedness, according to the gospel.

Read Proverbs 1:20-33, and chap 8:1-11, and chap. 9:1-6; Ezekiel 16:1-14; John 3:14-18, 36; Revelation 3:15-20. Here the Lord Jesus Christ stands knocking at the Laodiceans' door; he would happily have them to dine with him, and that he might dine with them; that is, that they might have intimate communion and fellowship one with another.

Now, pray tell me, what preparations or qualifications had these Laodiceans to entertain Christ? Surely none; for they were lukewarm, they were 'neither hot nor cold'; they were 'wretched, and miserable, and poor, and blind, and naked'; and yet Christ, to show his free grace and his condescending love, invites the very worst of sinners to open to him, though they were no ways so and so prepared or qualified to entertain him.

Remedy 3.

The third remedy against this device of Satan is, seriously to consider, that the Lord does not in all the Scripture require such and such prepar-

ations and qualifications before men come to
Christ, before they believe in Christ, or enter-
tain, or embrace the Lord Jesus.

Believing in Christ is the great thing that God presses upon sinners throughout the Scripture, as all know that know anything of Scripture.

Objection: But does not Christ say, 'Come unto me all ye that labour and are heavy laden, and I will give you rest'? (*Matt.* 11:28).

To this I shall give these three answers:

(i) That though the invitation be to such that 'labour and are heavy laden', yet the promise of giving rest is made over to 'coming', to 'believing'.

(ii) That all this scripture proves and shows is, that such as labour under sin as under a heavy burden, and that are laden with the guilt of sin and sense of God's displeasure, ought to come to Christ for rest; but it does not prove that only such must come to Christ, nor that all men must be thus burdened and laden with the sense of their sins and the wrath of God, before they come to Christ.

Poor sinners, when they are under the sense of sin and wrath of God, are prone to run from creature to creature, and from duty to duty, and from ordinance to ordinance, to find rest; and if they could find it in any thing or creature, Christ should never hear of them; but here the Lord sweetly invites them: and to encourage them, he engages himself to give them rest: 'Come', says Christ, 'and I will give you rest.' I will not *show* you rest, nor barely *tell* you of rest, but 'I will *give* you rest.' I am faithfulness itself, and cannot lie, 'I *will* give you rest.' I that have the greatest power to give it, the greatest will to give it, the greatest right to give it, 'Come, *laden sinners,* and I will give you rest.' Rest is the most desirable good, the most suitable good, and to you the greatest good. 'Come', says Christ, that is, 'believe in me, and I will give you rest'; I will give you peace with God, and peace with conscience; I will turn your storm into an everlasting calm; I will give you such rest, that the world can neither give to you nor take from you.

(iii) No one scripture speaks out the whole mind of God; therefore do but compare this one scripture with those several scriptures that are laid down in the second remedy last mentioned, and it will clearly appear, that though men are thus and thus burdened and laden with their sins and filled with horror and terror, if they may come to Christ, they may receive and embrace the Lord Jesus Christ.

REMEDY 4.

The fourth remedy against this device of Satan is, to consider, that all that trouble for sin, all that sorrow, shame, and mourning which is acceptable to God, and delightful to God, and prevalent with God, flows from faith in Christ, as the stream flows from the fountain, as the branch from the root, as the effect from the cause.

Zechariah 12:10: 'They shall look on him whom they have pierced, and they shall mourn for him.' All gospel mourning flows from believing; they shall first look, and then mourn. All that know anything know this, that 'whatsoever is not of faith is sin' (*Rom.* 14. 23). Till men have faith in Christ, their best services are but glorious sins.

DEVICE 4.

BY SUGGESTING TO A SINNER CHRIST'S UNWILLINGNESS TO SAVE.

*It is true, says Satan, Christ is able to save you,
but is he willing? Surely, though he is able,
yet he is not willing to save such a wretch as
you are, that have trampled his blood under
your feet, and that have been in open rebellion
against him all your days.*

Remedy 1.

First, the great journey that he has taken, from heaven to earth, on purpose to save sinners, strongly demonstrates his willingness to save them.

'I came not to call the righteous, but sinners to repentance.' (*Matt.* 9:13); 'This is a faithful saying, and worthy of all acceptation, that Christ Jesus came into the world to save sinners, of whom I am chief' (1 *Tim.* 1:15).

Remedy 2.

Secondly, his divesting himself of his glory in order to sinners' salvation, speaks out his willingness to save them.

He leaves his Father's bosom, he puts off his glorious robes, and lays aside his glorious crown, and bids *adieu* to his glistering courtiers the angels; and all this he does, that he may accomplish sinners' salvation.

Remedy 3.

Thirdly, that sea of sin, that sea of wrath, that sea of trouble, that sea of blood that Jesus Christ waded through, that sinners might be pardoned, justified, reconciled, and saved, strongly evidences his willingness to save sinners (2 Cor. 5:19-20).

Remedy 4.

Fourthly, his sending his ambassadors, early and late, to woo and entreat sinners to be reconciled to him, does with open mouth show his readiness and willingness to save sinners.

REMEDY 5.

Fifthly, his complaints against such as refuse him, and that turn their backs upon him, and that will not be saved by him, strongly declares his willingness to save them.

'He came to his own, and his own received him not' (*John* 1:11). So in John 5:40: 'But ye will not come to me, that ye may have life.'

REMEDY 6.

Sixthly, the joy and delight that he takes at the conversion of sinners demonstrates his willingness that they should be saved.

'I say unto you, that likewise joy shall be in heaven over one sinner that repenteth, more than over ninety and nine just persons that need no repentance' (*Luke* 15:7).

God the Father rejoices at the return of his prodigal son; Christ rejoices to see the travail of his soul; the Spirit rejoices that he has another temple to dwell in; and the angels rejoice that they have another brother to delight in (*Isa.* 53:11).

DEVICE 5.

BY WORKING A SINNER TO MIND MORE THE SECRET DECREES AND COUNSELS OF GOD, THAN HIS OWN DUTY.

What need you to busy yourself about receiving, embracing, and entertaining of Christ? says Satan; if you are elected, you shall be saved; if not, all that you can do will do you no good. Nay, he will work the soul not only to doubt of its election, but to conclude that he is not elected, and therefore, let him do what he can, he shall never be saved.

Remedy 1.

The first remedy against this device of Satan is, seriously to consider, that all the angels in heaven, nor all the men on earth, nor all the devils in hell, cannot tell to the contrary, but that you may be an elect person, a chosen vessel.

You may be confident of this, that God never made Satan one of his privy council, God never acquainted him with the names or persons of such that he has set his love upon to eternity.

Remedy 2.

The second remedy against this device of Satan is, to meddle with that which you have to do.

Secret things belong to the Lord, but revealed things belong to you (cf. *Deut.* 29: 29). Your work, sinner, is to be peremptory in believing, and in returning to the Lord; your work is to cast yourself upon Christ, lie at his feet, to wait on him in his ways; and to give him no rest till he shall say, 'Sinner, I am your portion, I am your salvation, and nothing shall separate between you and me.'

THOMAS BROOKS
A BRIEF BIOGRAPHY[1]

*I*f readers of Puritan literature were set the task of listing thirty of the 'mighties' among Puritan preachers, the name of Thomas Brooks would certainly appear among them, though few would be inclined to include him among 'the first three'. His name and his works are sufficiently esteemed to secure for him an enduring place in the hearts of knowledgeable Christians, and some few might even award him a topmost niche among the choicest spirits of the seventeenth century. His reputation as a writer of treatises for the heart has never been clouded. His literary style is always lively. Like many of his contemporaries

[1] By S. M. Houghton.

he drew his sermon-illustrations from the Scriptures themselves, from everyday life, and from ancient classical literature and history. The amalgam is invariably interesting and edifying.

Brooks is a preacher and writer whose biography, had it been written by himself or by a contemporary, would have possessed no small measure of interest. Unfortunately what can be gleaned of his life-story is scanty in the extreme. Alexander B. Grosart, in the Memoir printed in the Nichol's reprint of Brooks' Works (1866) spins it out to sixteen pages, but he had to search far and wide for elusive information, and the basic facts which he brings to light are few indeed. College and ecclesiastical records—all too brief can be supplemented by an occasional personal reference in Brooks' own writings, and Grosart, to his considerable joy, discovered and printed the Last Will and Testament of our Puritan. Then, too, Brooks' various treatises survive in their earliest editions and are dated. No portrait of him is known to exist. Of the man himself and his strong personality a clear picture is readily formed in the reader's mind. Our author lives in his writings. Apart from these he is a mere shadow.

Born in 1608—place and county unknown—he matriculated as a 'pensioner' at Emmanuel College, Cambridge, that 'nest of the Puritans', on the 7th July, 1625, the year of Charles I's accession to the throne of England and Scotland. The term 'pensioner' does not indicate poverty and there is reason to believe that the youth was the son of well-to-do parents. In Emmanuel College he would probably rub shoulders with such men as John Milton and the famed New England trio—Thomas Shepard, John Cotton, and Thomas Hooker. His love for and skill in Hebrew, Greek, and Latin was nurtured, if not inculcated, during his College days.

After 1625 the veil falls again and for twenty or more years nothing is known of our writer beyond the fact that, before he re-emerges from obscurity, he had become a preacher of the gospel. London seems to have been the sphere of his ministry. There is little doubt that he held strongly with the Parliamentary cause during the stormy Civil War (1642-48), and it is virtually certain that he acted as chaplain to Parliamentary commanders both on land and sea during this period. There is reason to think that he was on terms of some intimacy with Thomas Fairfax, the Commander-in-Chief of the Parliament's military forces. His horizons were greatly extended during these fateful years, for he lets fall the remark in one of his treatises that he had been abroad 'in other nations and countries'. And again: 'I have been some years at sea, and through grace I can say that I would not exchange my sea experiences for England's riches'. 'Some terrible storms I have been in', he adds.

By the end of the Civil War, Parliament or rather the New Model Army being victorious—Parliament and Army fell apart—Brooks was Preacher of the Gospel at Thomas Apostles, London. He was accounted sufficiently outstanding as a man of God to preach before the House of Commons (the Rump of the Long Parliament) in the same year (December 26). His sermon was afterwards published under the title, 'God's Delight in the Progress of the Upright', the text being Psalm 44:18: 'Our heart is not turned back, neither have our steps declined from thy way.' His second sermon before Parliament was preached on the 8th October, 1650, a thanksgiving day for Cromwell's victory over the Scots at Dunbar on September 3rd. On this occasion the text was, significantly, Isaiah 10:6, which we forbear to quote.

Two years later Brooks transferred from Thomas Apostles to another London Church, St Margaret's, Fish-Street Hill, not without much opposition from some members of his future congregation. Those who objected to his settlement complained that he had refused to administer the sacraments to certain folk whom he judged to be unworthy, an oblique testimony to Brooks' firmness of conscience. St Bartholomew's gloomy Day (1662) found him among the ministers evicted from their livings and driven into nonconformity. But he did not leave London, and apparently managed to reside and preach, as occasion offered, not far from St Margaret's. He escaped imprisonment, was eminent among ministers who refused to flee in the Year of Plague (1665), and was at his post to comfort the afflicted during and after the Great Fire of 1666. A lengthy treatise entitled *London's Lamentations* (based upon *Isa.* 42:24-25) appears in Vol. 6 of Brooks' *Works*. It runs to 312 pages and 'is perhaps the most remarkable contemporary memorial' of the calamitous event. It is described on its title-page as 'A serious discourse concerning that late fiery dispensation that turned our (once renowned) city into a ruinous heap: also the several lessons that are incumbent upon those whose houses have escaped the consuming flames.'

Little of a biographical nature remains to be added. The years 1652-80 were occupied by preaching and writing, a succession of treatises appearing at frequent intervals, of which *Precious Remedies against Satan's Devices* (1652) was the first. In 1676 his wife Martha (née Burgess) died. To her he bore the eloquent testimony: 'She was always best when she was most with God in a corner. She has many a whole day been pouring out her soul before God for the nation, for Sion, and the great concerns of her own soul, when them about her did judge it more expedient that she had been in her bed, by reason of some bodily infirmity that did hang upon her; but the divine pleasures that she took in her [corner] did drown the sense of pain.' We may judge that much of the success of Brooks' ministry assuredly resulted from his wife's support of him in prayer. Let Puritan wives be given their due; assuredly the 'price' of some of them was 'above rubies'. There seem to have been no children of the marriage.

After Martha's death three more years of life remained to Thomas. In the course of them he contracted a second marriage. His 'dear and honoured' second wife was a certain Patience Cartwright of whom he says that she made 'all relations to meet in one', by which we may judge that, despite her youthfulness (and perhaps because of it), she was a not unworthy successor to Martha. Six months after making his Will in March, 1680, Brooks entered into the joy of his Lord, gathered 'like as a shock of corn ascendeth in his season'.

Brooks' works certainly follow him. Not only did he serve his own generation by the will of God, but all generations since have seen reason to call him blessed. His writings have 'built up in their most holy faith' not a few of the Lord's stalwarts, besides the many who have made less impact on the church of God. An admixture of 'salt' (in the apostolic sense) has given outlet to their savour. The first printed work which Spurgeon gave to the church, his *Sermons* apart, was *Smooth Stones taken from Ancient*

Brooks, a compilation from Brooks' writings in the choosing of which his fiancée, Susannah Thompson, had collaborated. It may well be judged that something of the spiritual wealth of the 'heir of the Puritans' was derived from this quarter.

Grosart, in an Editorial Postscript which prefaces Vol. 6 of Brooks' *Works*, quotes Calamy as saying that our author was 'a very affecting preacher and useful to many'. To this sombre word of praise he adds his own weighty verdict: 'His slightest "Epistle" is "Bread of Life"; his most fugitive "Sermon" a full cup of "Living Water": . . . his one dominating aim to make dead hearts warm with the Life of the Gospel of Him who is Life; his supreme purpose to "bring near" the very Truth of God. Hence his directness, his urgency, his yearning, his fervour, his fulness of Bible citation, his wistfulness, his intensity, his emotion . . . His desire to be "useful" to souls, to achieve the holy success of serving Christ, to win a sparkling crown to lay at His feet, breathes and burns from first to last.'

Few who know Brooks' writings will wish to quarrel with Grosart. Our author is one of the select circle whose praise is 'in all churches of the saints', or at least in those churches which place value upon legacies of abiding spiritual worth. John Milton is often quoted as saying in his *Areopagitica* that 'a good book is the precious life-blood of a master spirit, embalmed and treasured up on purpose to a life beyond life.' Better still can we say of Thomas Brooks that, if not a master spirit, he possessed (which is of much greater worth) the *Spirit of his Master*.

OTHER BOOKS IN THE
POCKET PURITANS
SERIES

If you enjoyed reading this little book then you may
be interested to know that the Banner of Truth
Trust also publishes the six-volume set of Brooks'
Works (ISBN: 978 0 85151 302 7, approximately 600
pp. per volume, clothbound), and Brooks' *Precious
Remedies Against Stan's Devices* (ISBN: 978 0 85151
002 6, 254 pp. paperback) in the Puritan Paperback
series.

For more details of these and all other Banner
of Truth titles, please visit our website:

www.banneroftruth.co.uk

THE BANNER OF TRUTH TRUST

3 Murrayfield Road, 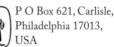 P O Box 621, Carlisle,
Edinburgh EH12 6EL Philadelphia 17013,
UK USA

www.banneroftruth.co.uk